Wild Canines

WOLVES

Holden Strauss

PowerKiDS press.
New York

Published in 2017 by The Rosen Publishing Group, Inc.
29 East 21st Street, New York, NY 10010

First Edition

Editor: Caitie McAneney
Book Design: Tanya Dellaccio

Photo Credits: Cover (wolf), p. 15 (moose, elk) Josef Pittner/Shutterstock.com; cover, pp. 3, 4, 6, 8–12, 14–16, 18–20, 22–24 (background) Iliveinoctober/Shutterstock.com; pp. 5, 11 (three gray wolves) Waddell Images/Shutterstock.com; p. 6 ArCaLu/Shutterstock.com; p. 7 David Osborn/Shutterstock.com; p. 8 Jean-Edouard Rozey/Shutterstock.com; p. 9 (Mexican gray wolf) Nagel Photography/Shutterstock.com; p. 9 (arctic wolf) Erni/Shutterstock.com; p. 9 (great plains wolf) Carol Heesen/Shutterstock.com; p. 9 (gray wolf) Dr. Alan Lipkin/Shutterstock.com; p. 11 (pack of wolves) Michael Roeder/Shutterstock.com; pp. 12, 22 Holly Kuchera/Shutterstock.com; pp. 13, 16 critterbiz/Shutterstock.com; p. 15 (wolf) kochanowski/Shutterstock.com; p. 17 schaef71/Shutterstock.com; p. 19 (arctic wolf) Denis Pepin/Shutterstock.com; p. 19 (three wolves) David Dirga/Shutterstock.com; p. 21 Jason Maehl/Getty Images.

Cataloging-in-Publication Data

Names: Strauss, Holden.
Title: Wolves / Holden Strauss.
Description: New York : PowerKids Press, 2017. | Series: Wild canines | Includes index.
Identifiers: ISBN 9781499420234 (pbk.) | ISBN 9781499420258 (library bound) | ISBN 9781499420241 (6 pack)
Subjects: LCSH: Wolves–Juvenile literature.
Classification: LCC QL737.C22 S745 2017 | DDC 599.74'442–d23

Manufactured in the United States of America

CPSIA Compliance Information: Batch #BS16PK: For Further Information contact Rosen Publishing, New York, New York at 1-800-237-9932

CONTENTS

Wild Wolves

Wolves are among the largest canines in the world. These wild canines look a lot like dogs. That's because **domesticated** dogs **descended** from wolves.

Wolves are often seen as dangerous, or unsafe. Many movies and books show them as **aggressive** towards people. In reality, wolves usually don't want to hurt people at all. These wild canines actually have a lot to teach us about living and working together as a team. Let's learn more about this amazing canine!

That's Wild!

Wolves are known for their nighttime calls to one another, which are called howls.

Gray wolves are the most common wolves in the world.

Wolves Up Close

A wolf's fur can be gray, tan, brown, black, reddish, or white. The color of a wolf's fur often depends on where it lives. Gray wolves blend in well with rocks and trees, while white Arctic wolves blend in with snow.

Wolves are different sizes. This also depends on where they live. Wolves that live in hot, dry areas, such as Ethiopian wolves, are small with light coats. Gray wolves that live in cold **regions** can grow to be over 130 pounds (59 kg) with thick coats!

Ethiopian wolf

That's Wild!

Wolves can mate, or make babies, with domesticated dogs. The result is called a wolf dog. Some people keep them as pets, but that's very dangerous.

The fur of gray wolves has two layers. The top coat is lighter and sheds water, and the inside coat is thick and warm.

Where Do Wolves Live?

Wolves used to live across the North American continent, as well as in regions of northern Europe, Asia, and eastern Africa. Today, their range is much smaller.

In North America, there are two main species, or kinds, of wolves. Gray wolves are the most common, while red wolves are **endangered**. Gray wolves live in the northern United States, as well as Alaska and Canada. Gray wolves also live in northern Asia, and a few still live in northern Europe. The red wolf lives in the southeastern United States.

red wolf

That's Wild!

There are only about 100 red wolves left in the wild. This species almost died out completely, but people have helped increase its population.

There are a number of subspecies, or smaller groups, of gray wolf. They include the Mexican wolf, Arctic wolf, Great Plains wolf, and the Rocky Mountain wolf.

The Wolf Pack

Many people use the term "lone wolf." However, wolves are almost never alone. They are very **social** animals, and they belong to a close family unit called a pack.

Packs have a social order, which means certain members are more powerful than others. The main male and female of the pack are the alpha couple. They're the only couple that can mate. Wolf packs hunt together, live together, and take care of young as a team. They **communicate** with each other using howls and other sounds.

That's Wild!

Wolves usually live in a pack of around six to ten members, but some wolf packs have up to 30 members!

Wolves howl for many reasons. A single wolf might howl to alert his pack. A wolf pack might howl to let other packs or predators know to stay away from their territory.

Wolf Pups

Usually, the alpha male and female mate once a year. They have a litter of one to 11 pups, or babies.

As the pups grow, all members of the wolf pack help to feed and raise them. Pups learn how to communicate with their pack. When they're around six months old, the pups are ready to join in the hunt. They follow their pack and learn important hunting skills by observing older wolves in action. Wolf pups also love to play!

That's Wild!

A wolf pack usually includes parents and their offspring, or young, but it can also include the pups' aunts and uncles.

The alpha female gives birth in a den, which is usually a cave, a hollow log, or a hole in the ground.

Big Eaters!

Wolves are big eaters. They sometimes eat smaller animals, such as birds, fish, snakes, and rabbits. However, when members of a wolf pack come together to hunt, they look for much bigger **prey**.

A successful hunt for a wolf pack might land them a deer or elk. They might also catch a caribou or moose. Other large meals might include huge bison or musk oxen. A wolf can eat up to 20 pounds (9 kg) of meat in one sitting!

That's Wild!

Each pack might prefer to hunt a certain kind of prey. For example, one pack might be skilled in taking down moose. Another pack may have their own skills for killing elk.

Wolf packs often target large animals with hooves.

Pack Hunting

Every wolf in the pack has a part to play in the hunt. The pack cooperates, or works together, to plan the attack.

Wolves don't **ambush** their prey. A hunt can take days. The pack might follow a herd. They watch the herd and find the weakest member. The wolf pack looks at the weather and land conditions when planning an attack. When the time is right, several members of the pack strike their target.

That's wild!
A wolf can spring forward at nearly 40 miles (64.4 km) per hour.

A wolf's sharp teeth and strong jaws can snap through huge bones!

Amazing Adaptations

Over time, wolves have **adapted** to their surroundings. They've adapted so well that they're usually the top predator in their **habitat**.

Wolves have great senses of hearing, sight, and smell. Wolves who live in colder regions have thick fur that helps them survive in low temperatures. The best wolf adaptation is their ability to communicate and cooperate as a team. Wolf packs look after one another so predators can't attack. Packs can also take down larger prey than a single wolf could.

That's Wild!

Wolves around the world have special adaptations that help them survive temperatures from -70 degrees Fahrenheit (-57 degrees Celsius) to 120 degrees Fahrenheit (49 degrees Celsius).

Arctic wolves have white fur, which is an adaptation that helps them blend in with their snowy surroundings. This adaptation is called camouflage.

Wolves and People

Many people see wolves as big and bad. However, wolves don't want to hurt people at all. They try to stay away from people as much as possible. In fact, over the past 100 years in North America, there have been only two deadly wolf attacks. That number is far smaller than the number of deadly attacks by pet dogs.

People are a bigger risk to wolves. People have pushed wolves out of their native habitats. In the 1800s and early 1900s, people were given prizes for killing wolves. Wolf populations were wiped out in many regions of North America.

That's Wild!

Many people killed wolves because they thought wolves attacked livestock, or farm animals. While some wolves have attacked livestock, this isn't as common as people thought.

Hunters killed all of the wolves in Yellowstone National Park. In 1995, wolves were brought back to the park, which affected the **ecosystem** there for the better.

The Truth About Wolves

Around the world, wolves are often seen as aggressive and dangerous toward people. Now you know that's far from the truth.

Many wolf populations are at risk. The red wolf, Mexican wolf, and Ethiopian wolf are seriously endangered. Wolves are important to their ecosystems. They keep prey populations from getting too high. These amazing animals form friendships, and they love to hunt, play, and howl together. They take care of sick, old, or hurt members of their pack. We have a lot to learn from wolves!

Glossary

adapt: To change in order to live better in a certain environment.

aggressive: Showing a readiness to attack.

ambush: A surprise attack.

communicate: To share ideas and feelings through sounds and motions.

descend: To come down from a source.

domesticated: Bred and raised for use by people.

ecosystem: All the living things in an area.

endangered: In danger of dying out.

habitat: The natural place where an animal or plant lives.

prey: An animal hunted by other animals for food.

region: A large area of land that has a number of features in common.

social: Tending to form relationships with others.

Index

Websites

Due to the changing nature of Internet links, PowerKids Press has developed an online list of websites related to the subject of this book. This site is updated regularly. Please use this link to access the list:
www.powerkidslinks.com/canine/wolf